MW01282354

by
Adam Balest

edited by CJC

Copyright © 2017 Adam Balest

ISBN: 1979566208
ISBN-13: 978-1979566209

DEDICATION

To Elena, the most beautiful part of me.

CONTENTS

TODAY'S TIDES

Wonderful blue aged morning -
      my language spelled out for me.

    Interactive every moments -
      evenly create my experience.

    Asleep, slumber, all the feelings of today's tides -
      changing every other yes and why.

INTERIOR ART

Desert flowers in vase.
A still life in reality, taking space and taking shape.
It's colors, a burnt yellow and warmly crimson.
Distilled down to the echo of intent.
Standing dry, indoors and insight.
Someone waters this dead thing.
A rotting effigy as interior art.

It creates atmosphere.

CIRCLE

Practice becomes ritual.
    The ritual is the practice.

THE TRAPS

Feeling separate from the rest,
rhythmic movement of the masses
boring me to death.

Left searching through cleansed doors,
my mind goes looking
through the traps in the floors.

DEVICES TO TIME OURSELVES

From underneath the water to over land -
space stands in our mental projections
hourglasses and clock hands.

COOLED

My cell phone tones in even blips of threes.

Summer time relations cooled by mint tea.

Open window Sunday, naked on a breeze.

NEVER WAVER

These trials of the brain
    left standing in the rain.

Never wavering or bending
    in or outside the game.

AN ART

Living is an art,
and a matter of perspective.

SNAIL'S RACE

The traffic crawls on and on,
similar to a snail's race.

OUR PARTS

Your eyes, my mind -
all of our parts equally meeting in a dispatch of words and
gestures.

Both physical and mental,
all the way.

OPEN

The heat rises as the cock croons a morning cry.

Desert winds scatter the arid heat on all living things.

Blistered and burnt, torn steel sheets lie rusted here and there. It is a waste land, with real estate prices growing.

A lone dove befriended. Thirsty as it looks
towards humans
who have shelter from the elements.

The door is open, but it won't come in.

ZOO LIFE

Captive in a concrete jungle with visitors eyes panorama.
Heart over matter filled with straw and hay.

The ladies sleep and mingle on ancient pelts that represent
the height of human leisure.

Toppling the king of beasts into beaten rugs.
Stained, not with blood, but wine.

WINE IN HAND

Meeting of the minds,
    foul play, or four?

Interesting conversations -
    maintaining eye contact.
Hands still, keep them there.

Music overhead,
    wine in hand.

The temperature fluctuates
    with the success of our dialogue.

Do you read Hume or Aristotle?

Nothing like a polished topic -
    to get the blood boiling.

A perfect innuendo.

THE FOREST

The forest, a perpetual state of becoming.

Inland lives barren of fresh air,
    cement their names in drying concrete.

There is no night sky.
    Only the half-moon waxing through haze of pollution
        and agoraphobia.

GREET YOURSELF

It's good to greet yourself when you look into the mirror.

With a blazing smile of self love, you can provide self assurance every day.

Set the example of how you want others to treat you.

Live the Golden Rule through yourself, with love and acceptance.

HAIKU #1

Breath taken deeply,
    in as much as I can take.
Some things never change.

HAIKU #2

Nothing ever stops.
    The spirit moves in circles.
Loves equal ghosting.

HAIKU #3

Curving roads at night.
　　His hands gripped the wheel tightly.
The unknown ahead.

NOT A LIE

Spinning everyday, so fast it blurs our lives.

Filling each day with endless moments of time.

We may try to grasp the sand, but the grains fall no matter how tightly we hold on.

The only thing that is not a lie, is that we are all going to die.

WHAT LASTS FOREVER

Searching for what lasts forever.

The paw of an animal touching your hand,
no claws extended.

The hand of a child touching your finger,
trust cemented.

The lips of a lover, touching your breath,
all love lamented.

Let love carry you through the suffering.

When you die with love and happiness, you've found what
lasts forever.

LET LOVE IN

Let love into every aspect of your life.

Enable love's universal feeling to synchronize yourself
with
the heartbeat of reality.

There is no way to avoid suffering if you do not love.

Love can save everyone,
one by one.
Love can save everything,
all is one.

One and all...

AUTHOR

Adam Balest is a multi-faceted artist utilizing the mediums of prose, poetry, film, music and technology to express himself. He strives to write poems that contain both a philosophical and emotional element. A tired optimist, he continues to hope that humanity will universally love one another and live by the Golden Rule.

Made in the USA
Las Vegas, NV
17 July 2022